# PRACTICAL INDONESIAN

## a communication guide

### by JOHN BARKER

PERIPLUS

Published by Periplus Editions (HK) Ltd.

**Distributors:**
*Asia Pacific*
Berkeley Books Pte Ltd
130 Joo Seng Road, 06-01/03
Singapore 368357
Tel: (65) 6280 1330 Fax: (65) 6280 6290

*Indonesia*
PT. Java Books Indonesia
Jl. Gading Kirana I, Blok A14 No.17
Kelapa Gading Kirana
Jakarta 14240
Tel: (021) 451 5351 Fax: (021) 453 4987

Sixteenth Printing, July 2004
Printed in Indonesia
**ISBN 0-945971-52-4**

ACKNOWLEDGEMENT: Many thanks to A. Hutagalung and P. Balachandran, who assisted greatly with the Indonesian and Malaysian translations respectively.

# FOREWORD

### About the language and this book

As any seasoned traveler knows, the ability to communicate in the language of the country you are visiting makes a very big difference in the experiences you have. Even a basic grasp of a few essentials will help you to relate to the people, get where you want to go, pay the right prices, and get much more out of your visit.

That's the reason for this book, which is designed especially for travelers to Indonesia and Malaysia. The emphasis is on effective communication, not grammar rules or tourist phrases. It is organized to be as simple, concise, and useful as possible. With this book and a few hours of practice you can start communicating in Indonesian/Malay.

The main focus of this book is Indonesia and Indonesian, simply because here is where the greatest need exists. (In Malaysia English is spoken fairly widely.) At the same time, Indonesian and Malay are in fact regional variations of the same language, so why not kill the proverbial two birds? And making use of your Malay in Malaysia will make your visit there infinitely more rewarding.

So, the book itself is written with Indonesia and Bahasa Indonesia in mind. I have marked° the text and included an appendix to make conversion to Malay (where necessary) a painless, easy step. If you pass from Indonesia into Malaysia, or vice versa, just refer to this appendix and to the glossary.

*Using this book:* Begin by going over the pronunciation and grammar guides briefly, returning to them as needed. Then on to the basics: greetings, time and numbers. The rest of the book offers sections dealing with situations and activities you'll be part of. The three special sections are designed for easy reference to especially useful information. A glossary and the Malay appendix complete the guide.

Good luck and good traveling. *Selamat jalan*!

# CONTENTS

# PRONUNCIATION GUIDE

Proper pronounciation is important. Often a word that is slightly mispronounced is just not understood. If possible we suggest you go over this section (and other words in the book) with a native speaker. Try to imitate his or her pronounciation as closely as you can.

### Sentence stress
As in English, the most important word in a sentence is stressed. Unlike English, the most important word is often placed first. The rhythm tends to be staccato.

### Syllable stress
As a rule the **second to last** syllable is stressed: *BU-ku* (book), *sau-DA-ra* (you). Exception: If the **second to last** syllable contains an 'e', stress is on the **last** syllable: *per-GI* (go), *be-LUM* (not yet).

### Vowel sounds
a       like **a** in father: *dekat*/near, *apa*/what, *bisa*/can

e       is pronounced three different ways:
        1) like unstressed **e** (schwa): *pelan*/slow
        2) like **é** in passé: *sore*/afternoon
        3) like **è** in bet or ten: *teh*/tea

i       usually like **i** in Bali: *hari*/day, *lihat*/see, *ibu*/mother. But when enclosed by consonants, like **i** in sit: *minta*/request, *pintu*/door

| | |
|---|---|
| o | Like **o** in n**o**: *sore*/afternoon, *nomor*/number, *toko*/shop: |
| u | like **ou** in y**ou**: *satu*/one, *duduk*/sit |
| ai | like **i** in line: *kain:*/cloth, *baik*/good, *pantai*/beach |
| au | like **ow** in h**ow**: *atau*/or, *kalau*/if |

## Consonant sounds

In general, the pronounciation of consonants is the same as in English. Here are the exceptions:

| | |
|---|---|
| c | always like **ch** in **ch**air: *cinta*/ to love, *cuci*/to wash |
| g | always hard like **g** in **g**arden: *tiga*/three, *gila*/crazy |
| h | 1) at the beginning of a word, is very soft: *habis*/finish, *haus*/thirsty |
| | 2) between like vowels, is very strong: *mahal*/expensive, *pohon*/tree |
| | 3) between different vowels, is very soft: *lihat*/to see, *tahun*/year |
| | 4) at the end of a word, is very soft: *sudah*/already, *teh*/tea |
| k | 1) at the beginning or middle of a word, like **k** in **k**iss: *kunci*/key, *buku*/book |
| | 2) at end of word is "glottal stop", not fully pronounced: *tidak*/no, *rokok*/cigarette |
| r | like a Spanish **r**, rolled: *kamar*/room, *ramai*/crowded |

| | |
|---|---|
| **ng** | soft, like **ng** in si**ng**er: *mengerti*/to understand |
| **ngg** | hard, like **ng** in si**ng**le: *tinggal*/to stay |
| **ny** | like **ny** in la**ny**ard: *banyak*/many, much; *nyonya*/Mrs. |
| **kh** | like **k** but harder: *khabar*/news |

**Note on spelling**
In 1972 certain changes were made to standardize Indonesian and Malay spellings:

| Old spelling | New spelling |
|---|---|
| tj | c |
| j | y |
| dj | j |
| ch | kh |

You still see a variety of different spellings, however, on signs and forms.

For purposes of basic communication Indonesian grammar is much easier than that of English. Unlike English, Indonesian has **NO:**

1. Articles. The words: **the, a, an** have no equivalents and are often omitted. I don't have **a** room = *Saya tidak ada kamar* = I don't have room; They enter **the** room = *Mereka masuk kamar* = They enter room.

2. Verb "to be." The copula "to be" is not usually translated: This book **is** good = *Buku ini baik* = This book good; They **are** nice = *Mereka baik* = They nice.

3. Plural form. Sometimes a noun is repeated to form the plural (*buku-buku*/books), but as a rule the singular form expresses both one or many. Plurality is indicated by the context or by words like: all/*semua*, many/*banyak*, etc. **Note:** Often a doubled word has a different meaning from the word alone: *mata* = eye but *mata-mata* = spy.

4. Comparatives (-er, -est). The words more/*lebih* and most/*paling* are used before adjectives: good, better, best = *baik, lebih baik, paling baik*; cheap, cheaper, cheapest = *murah, lebih murah, paling murah*.

5. Verb tenses. Indonesian verbs are not conjugated. Will go, going, went and gone all translate as *pergi*. Past, continuous, perfect and future tenses are indicated

by the sentence context, or by such words as yesterday, already, later, will, etc. Here are some examples:

| | | |
|---|---|---|
| **Past** | *kemarin*/yesterday | Yesterday I went to Ubud. = *Kemarin saya pergi ke Ubud.* |
| | *yang lalu*/ago | I came two hours ago. = *Saya datang dua jam yang lalu.* |
| **Perfect** | *sudah*/already | He has gone. = He already go. = *Dia sudah pergi.* |
| **Future** | *akan*/will (shall) | When will she come? |
| | *mau*/will (want to) | = *Kapan dia akan datang* or *Kapan dia mau datang?* |
| | *besok*/tomorrow | Tomorrow we will see. = Tomorrow we see. = *Besok kita lihat.* |

**Note on prefixes/suffixes.** In Indonesian, new forms are derived from root words by adding prefixes (*me-, per-, ber-, di-, ter-*) and suffixes (*-i, -an, -kan*). The rules for these are complex and confusing. Fortunately, for basic communication you can just use the root word (as do many Indonesians in everyday conversation).

## PERSONAL PRONOUNS

| I | *saya, aku* | (*saya* is more common) |
|---|---|---|
| we | *kita* | (**including** the person addressed) |
| | *kami* | (**excluding** the person addressed |
| you | *anda, saudara* | (polite forms for general use) |
| | *kamu* | (use only with friends and children) |
| he/she | *dia* | |
| they | *mereka* | |

**Note:** see also the **Forms of Address** section, next page.

## POSSESSIVES

Just place the appropriate pronoun right after any noun to express possession. You can also use endings for my, your and his/her, as shown:

| my house | *rumah saya* or *rumahku* | (*-ku* = my) |
|---|---|---|
| our car | *mobil kita* | (inclusive) |
| | *mobil kami* | (exclusive) |
| your name | *nama kamu* | (informal) |
| | *nama saudara* | (more polite) |
| | *namamu* | (*-mu* = your) |

| his/her ticket | *karcis dia* or |
| | *karcisnya* (-*nya* = his/her) |
| their money | *uang mereka* |

**Grammar note: It** and **its**. There is no direct translation for these. In some cases the word 'it' is omitted; often it is expressed as "this" or "that" (*ini* or *itu*), or sometimes the -*nya* ending is used. In the examples we employ the different terms as appropriate, but as a rule you can just keep repeating the noun or use this/*ini* or that/*itu* if the object is understood.

## FORMS OF ADDRESS

**All in the Family:** In Indonesian, family terms are commonly applied to everyone. The word "*bapak*" (father) is used as "Mr" and "*ibu*" (mother) as "Mrs" when addressing older people. Younger people are referred to as "brother" or "sister."

| Father | *Bapak* ("*Pak*") |
| Mother | *Ibu* ("*Bu*") |
| Elder brother | *Abang* ("*Bang*" or "*Bung*") or *Mas* (in Java only) |
| Elder sibling | *Kakak* ("*Kak*") |
| Younger brother or sister | *Adik* ("*Dik*") |

## OTHER TERMS USED

| | |
|---|---|
| *Tuan* | for a highly respected foreigner |
| *Nona°* | Miss, an unmarried woman |
| *Nyonya°* | Mrs, married woman of high standing |

Professional titles, such as doctor/*dokter*, professor, etc. — as in English.

---

**NOTE:** ° indicates different Malay usage — refer to the appendix at the back.

---

**Notes on usage:**

1. In most situations, it is better to use "family" forms of address or a person's proper name instead of the pronoun "you." For example, if you are speaking to an older woman: Where are **you** going? = Where is **mother** (*ibu*) going? = ***Ibu** pergi ke mana?* This style of address is more polite and therefore preferred.

2. The pronoun *kamu* for "you" is reserved to address close friends or social inferiors. The word *anda* is more neutral, and has recently become popular. *Saudara*, literally "brother (or sister)" is also used as a polite form of "you" to address people who are about the same age.

3. The terms *Bu, Pak, Nona* and *Nyonya* are very often used in conjunction with first names: *Bu* Purwo, *Pak* Prawoto, etc. The same applies to titles.

# STATEMENTS & QUESTIONS

WORD ORDER

The same as in English: subject-verb-object. As a rule, however, the main (most important) word comes first, the rest follows. As you'll see, sentences tend to be short, since many parts of speech used in English can be omitted and dependent clauses are not commonly found.

Adjectives directly follow the noun they modify:

| expensive batik | *batik mahal* |
| big store | *toko besar* |

Exceptions are the adjectives all, many, few:

| all | *semua* |
| All losmen are cheap. | *Semua losmen murah.* |
| many/much | *banyak* |
| many friends | *banyak teman* |
| few/a little | *sedikit* |
| a little money | *sedikit uang* |

QUESTIONS

There are three ways to form questions:

1. Rising voice inflection only:
   You are going now?   *Saudara pergi sekarang?*

2. *Apakah* at the beginning of the sentence:
   Are you hungry?   *Apakah saudara lapar?*

3. Use a question word:
   **Why?**   ***Kenapa* ?**
   Why am I here?   *Kenapa saya ada disni?*

**How?** *Bagaimana?*
How can I go there? *Bagaimana saya bisa ke sana?*

**How much/many?** *Berapa*
How much (long) time ? *Berapa lama?*
How much (price) is this? *Berapa harga ini?*
NOTE: What time is it?
= "How many hours now?" *Jam berapa sekarang?*

**What?** *Apa?*
What is this? *Apa ini?*

**Where?** *Mana?*
Where is it? *Mana itu?*
Where are they going? *Mereka ke mana?*

**Who?** *Siapa?*
Who's that? *Siapa itu?*
NOTE: What's your name?
= "Who is your name?" *Siapa nama saudara?*

**When?** *Kapan°?*
When did he go? *Kapan dia pergi?*

REQUESTS

**May** *Boleh*
May I enter? *Boleh saya masuk?*

**Please give me** *Minta*
Please give me some drinking water.
*Minta air minum.*

# NUMBERS

| | | | | | |
|---|---|---|---|---|---|
| 1 | *satu* | 6 | *enam* | **teen = *belas*** | |
| 2 | *dua* | 7 | *tujuh* | 11 | *sebelas* |
| 3 | *tiga* | 8 | *delapam* | 12 | *dua belas* |
| 4 | *empat* | 9 | *sembilan* | 13 | *tiga belas* |
| 5 | *lima* | 10 | *sepuluh* | | etc. |

## tens = *puluh*

| | | | |
|---|---|---|---|
| 20 | *dua puluh* | 50 | *lima puluh* |
| 30 | *tiga puluh* | 60 | *enam puluh* |
| 31 | *tiga puluh satu* (3-10-1) | 70 | *tujuh puluh* |
| 32 | *tiga puluh dua* (3-10-2) | 80 | *delapan puluh* |
| 40 | *empat puluh* | 90 | *sembilan puluh* |

## hundreds = *ratus*                ## thousands = *ribu*

| | | | |
|---|---|---|---|
| 100 | *seratus* | 1 000 | *seribu* |
| 200 | *dua ratus* | 2 000 | *dua ribu* |
| 300 | *tiga ratus* | 10 000 | *sepuluh ribu* |
| | etc. | 100 000 | *seratus ribu* |
| | | | etc. |

## million = *juta*

1 000 000   *satu juta*
2 000 000   *dua juta*, etc.

| | | | |
|---|---|---|---|
| $\frac{1}{2}$ | *setengah* | first | *pertama* |
| $\frac{1}{4}$ | *seperempat* | second | *kedua* |
| $\frac{3}{4}$ | *tiga per empat* | third | *ketiga* |
| $1\frac{1}{2}$ | *satu setengah* | fourth | *keempat* etc. |

## USEFUL WORDS

| | |
|---|---|
| number | *nomor* |
| total quantity | *jumlah* |
| plus | *tambah* |
| minus | *kurang* |
| approximately | *kira-kira* |
| how many/much | *berapa* |
| many/much | *banyak* |
| few/a little | *sedikit* |
| enough | *cukup* |
| more (quantity) | *lagi* |
| too | *terlalu* |
| too many | *terlalu banyak* |
| too little | *terlalu sedikit* |

# TIME

## VOCABULARY

| | | | |
|---|---|---|---|
| minute | *menit* | today | *hari ini* |
| hour | *jam°* (also: "clock, watch") | tomorrow | *besok* |
| | | yesterday | *kemarin°* |
| week | *minggu* | now | *sekarang* |
| month | *bulan* (also "moon") | in a moment | *sebentar* |
| | | later | *nanti* |
| year | *tahun* | earlier | *tadi* |
| date | *tanggal* | ago | *yang lalu* |
| | | just now | *baru saja* |

**Time of day**

| | |
|---|---|
| *pagi-pagi* | 5-7 am |
| *pagi* | 7-11 am |
| *siang* | 11 am-3 pm |
| *sore°* | 3-7 pm |
| *malam* | night (dark hours) |

**Days of the week**

| | |
|---|---|
| Sunday | *Hari Minggu* |
| Monday | *Hari Senen* |
| Tuesday | *Hari Selasa* |
| Wednesday | *Hari Rabu* |
| Thursday | *Hari Kamis* |
| Friday | *Hari Jum'at* |
| Saturday | *Hari Sabtu* |

## TELLING TIME

| | |
|---|---|
| What time is it? | *Jam berapa?°* |
| (It's) 9 o'clock. | *Jam sembilan.°* |
| (It's) 7:30. | *Jam setengah delapan.°* (= half eight) |
| (It's) 2:45. | *Jam tiga kurang seperempat.°* (= three less a quarter) |
| (It's) 8:10. | *Jam delapan lewat sepuluh .* (= ten past eight) |

(It's) "rubber time"!     *Jam karet!*
(Good for a laugh when you are late.)

**Note:**   What time is it?     *Jam berapa?*
                 How many hours?     *Berapa jam?*

USEFUL PHRASES

| | |
|---|---|
| What day is it now? | *Hari apa sekarang?* |
| Monday. | *Hari Senen.* |
| | |
| What's the date today? | *Tanggal berapa hari ini?* |
| It's January 1. | *Tanggal 1 Januari.* |
| | |
| When did you arrive? | *Kapan saudara datang?* |
| I just arrived. | *Saya baru saja datang.* |
| Earlier this morning | *Tadi pagi.* |
| Three days ago | *Tiga hari yang lalu.* |
| | |
| When are you leaving? | *Kapan saudara berangkat?* |
| Later this afternoon. | *Nanti sore.* |
| Tomorrow afternoon. | *Besok sore.* |
| In a little while. | *Sebentar lagi.* |

**Note:**   time (in a general sense)     *waktu*
                 time (length of)     *lama*
                 times (e.g. many times)     *kali*

# GREETINGS & CIVILITIES

"HELLO" AND "GOODBYE"

The English words "hello" and "bye-bye" are now also used in Indonesian, but the traditional greetings are:

| | |
|---|---|
| *Selamat datang* | Welcome |
| *Selamat pagi* | Good morning |
| *Selamat siang* | Good midday |
| *Selamat sore* | Good afternoon |
| *Selamat malam* | Goodnight |
| *Selamat tidur* | Have a good sleep |
| *Selamat jalan* | Goodbye ("good journey," said to someone leaving) |
| *Selamat tinggal* | Goodbye ("good stay," said to someone staying) |

**Note:** *Selamat* is a word of Arabic origin that literally means "May your time/action be blessed."

"HOW ARE YOU" / "I'M FINE"

| | |
|---|---|
| *Apa khabar?* | How are you? (lit: "What's the news?") |
| *Khabar baik* | Fine. (lit: "The news is fine.") |

"PLEASE"

There are different ways to translate the word "please" in Indonesian and foreigners very often confuse them:

1) ***Minta***    Literally "to ask for;" used when ordering something.

| *Minta taxi.* | A taxi, please. |
|---|---|

2) **Tolong**   Literally "to help;" used when asking for assistance.

*Tolong kasih tahu saya.*   Please let me know.

3) **Coba**   Literally "to try;" used in the sense of "please let me" [have a look, etc.].

*Coba lihat itu.*   Please let me see that.

4) **Mari**   An invitational, meaning: "let's go, please go ahead."

*Mari, makan.*   Let's eat.
*Mari, duduk..*   Please sit down.

5) **Silahkan**   Similar to *mari*, meaning "go ahead," often used in response to a request.

*Boleh saya duduk?*   May I sit down?
*Silahkan.*   Please, go ahead.

## "THANK YOU" / "YOU'RE WELCOME"

| *Terima kasih* | Thank you. |
|---|---|
| *Kembali* | You're welcome (lit: "return") |
| *Sama-sama* | You're welcome (lit: "same to you") |

## "EXCUSE ME"

| *Ma'af* | Excuse me ("I'm sorry, pardon me"). |
|---|---|
| *Permisi* | Excuse me (used when taking one's leave, but not on a trip). |

# SIMPLE WORDS & SENTENCES: I

| | | | |
|---|---|---|---|
| and | *dan* | this/these | *ini* |
| or | *atau* | that/those | *itu* |
| with | *dengan* | more | *lebih* |
| for | *untuk* | less | *kurang* |
| good | *bagus* | better | *lebih baik* |
| nice, fine | *baik* | bad/worse | *kurang baik* |
| yes | *ya* | very | *sekali* |
| no, not | *tidak* | different | *lain* |
| not | *bukan** | same | *sama* |

**Note:** *tidak* is used with verbs, adjectives, adverbs.
*bukan* is used with nouns and pronouns.

| | | | |
|---|---|---|---|
| to be, have | *ada* | can, be able | *bisa°* |
| to own | *punya* | to get | *dapat* |
| to like | *suka* | to know | *tahu* |
| to want | *mau* | to take | *ambil* |
| to need | *perlu* | to see | *lihat* |
| to buy | *beli* | to sell | *jual* |

| | |
|---|---|
| Are there (any) rooms? | *Ada kamar?* |
| Sorry, there aren't (any). | *Ma'af, tidak ada.* |
| | |
| What (do you) want? | *Mau apa?* |
| I need that. | *Saya perlu itu.* |
| I want to buy this. | *Saya mau beli ini.* |
| I need two more. | *Saya perlu dua lagi.* |
| | |
| (Is) this good or not? | *Ini bagus tidak?* |
| Those (are) not so good. | *Itu kurang bagus.* |

These (are) very good.  *Ini bagus sekali.*
Yes, but these (are) better.  *Ya, tetapi ini lebih bagus.*

Not that (one)!  *Bukan itu!*

(Is it) the same or different?  *Ini sama atau lain?*
I don't know.  *Saya tidak tahu.*

May I take one?  *Boleh saya ambil satu?*
Please, take two.  *Mari, ambil dua.* (or)
  *Silahkan ambil dua.*

(Do you) want to go
with him?  *Mau pergi sama dia?*
No, (I) don't want (to).  *Tidak mau.*

Can (you) see (it)?  *Bisa lihat?*
Yes, (I) can.  *Ya, bisa.*

Who is this for?  *Ini untuk siapa?* (or)
  *Untuk siapa, ini?*
I like it.  *Saya suka itu.*

**Note:** Words in parentheses ( ) are not used in the Indonesian translation.

| | | | |
|---|---|---|---|
| if | *kalau, jika* | to speak | *bicara°* |
| but | *tetapi* | to tell | *bilang°* |
| then | *lalu, kemudian* | to ask | *tanya* |
| only | *hanya, saja* | to understand | *mengerti* |
| correct | *betul* | to go | *pergi* |
| wrong | *salah* | to wait | *tunggu* |
| from | *dari* | to give | *kasih* |
| | | | |
| big | *besar* | already | *sudah* |
| small | *kecil* | not yet | *belum* |
| beautiful | *cantik* | old | *tua, lama* |
| slow(ly) | *pelan(-pelan)* | new | *baru* |
| fast | *cepat* | the one which | *yang\** |

**\*Note:** *Yang* is a relative pronoun with many uses:

| | | |
|---|---|---|
| *yang kecil* | = | the small one |
| *yang ini* | = | this one |
| *yang mana?* | = | which one? |
| *bis° yang baru* | = | the new bus |
| *gadis yang cantik* | = | the beautiful girl |

| | |
|---|---|
| I don't understand. | *Saya tidak mengerti.* |
| I can't speak Indonesian. | *Saya tidak bisa bicara Bahasa Indonesia.* |
| Please speak slowly. | *Tolong bicara pelan-pelan.* |
| Wait, I will ask. | *Tunggu, saya akan tanya.* |
| Please tell me. | *Tolong bilang kepada saya.* |

| | |
|---|---|
| Please give me that. | *Tolong kasih saya itu.* |
| (Is) this new or old? | *Ini baru atau lama?* |
| Where is this from? | *Ini dari mana?* |
| This bus (is) small, but that one (is) big. | *Bis° ini kecil, tetapi yang itu besar.* |
| Which one do you want? | *Anda mau yang mana?* |
| I only want this one. | *Saya hanya mau yang ini.* |
| | (or) *Saya mau yang ini saja.* |

I want the new one.      *Saya mau yang baru.*
( = I want the one which [is] new.)

| | |
|---|---|
| (Is) that right or not? | *Itu betul tidak?* |
| No, that (is) wrong. | *Tidak, itu salah.* |
| How many (do you) already have? | *Sudah punya berapa?* |
| Not (yet) enough. | *Belum cukup.* |
| I (shall) wait 10 minutes, then I shall go | *Saya tunggu sepuluh menit, lalu saya akan pergi.* |
| Have you eaten yet? | *Sudah makan, belum?* |
| Yes, I have. | *Sudah.* |
| No, not yet. | *Belum.* |

# GETTING AROUND

| | | | |
|---|---|---|---|
| at | *di* | to stay | *tinggal* |
| to | *ke* | to go | *pergi* |
| from | *dari* | to stop | *berhenti* |
| where | *mana* | to come, arrive | *datang* |
| | | | |
| here | *sini* | to depart | *berangkat* |
| there | *sana* | to return | *kembali* |
| near | *dekat* | to walk | *berjalan,* |
| far | *jauh* | | *jalan kaki* |
| | | | |
| over there | *di situ* | by (means of) | *naik* |
| via | *lewat* | place | *tempat* |
| | | | |
| road, way | *jalan* | bicycle | *sepeda°* |
| alley | *gang* | motorcycle | *sepeda motor°* |
| car | *mobil°* | rent, hire | *sewa* |

| | |
|---|---|
| Where is he? | *Di mana dia?* |
| Far from here. | *Jauh dari sini.* |
| (It) is there. | *Ada di sana.* |
| | |
| Where (are you) going? | *Pergi ke mana?* (or) |
| | *Mau ke mana?\** |
| I am going to Bali. | *Saya pergi ke Bali.* |
| | |
| Where (have you come) from? | *Dari mana?* |
| I have just come from Jakarta. | *Saya baru datang dari Jakarta.* |

| | |
|---|---|
| Where (are you) staying? | *Tinggal di mana?* |
| Over there. In a hotel. | *Di situ. Di hotel.* |
| | |
| How (did you) come? | *Datang naik apa?* |
| By car. | *Naik mobil.* |
| By motorcycle. | *Naik sepeda motor.* |
| | |
| How will you go? | *Mau pergi naik apa?* |
| If (it's) close, I'll walk. | *Kalau dekat, saya jalan kaki.* |
| | |
| Stop here. | *Berhenti di sini.* |
| | |
| I came yesterday. | *Saya datang kemarin.* |
| I depart tomorrow. | *Saya berangkat besok.* |
| I will return later. | *Saya akan kembali nanti.* |

**\*Note:** the word *mau* (to want) is often used in place of *pergi* (to go): I go to Bali = *Saya mau ke Bali.*

# PUBLIC TRANSPORT

| | | | |
|---|---|---|---|
| terminal | *terminal* | seat | *tempat (duduk)* |
| station | *setasiun°* | direct | *langsung* |
| ticket | *karcis°* | express | *expres* |
| ticket | | agent | *agen* |
|   window | *loket°* | fast | *cepat* |
| airport | *airport,* | slow(-ly) | *pelan(-pelan)* |
| | *bandar udara* | full | *penuh* |
| airplane | *pesawat* | empty | *kosong* |
| ship | *kapal laut* | crowded | *ramai* |
| train | *kereta api* | still | *masih* |
| bus | *bis°* | class | *kelas* |
| night bus | *bis malam* | comfortable, | |
| taxi | *taksi* |   nice | *enak* |
| pedicab | *becak* | cancel | *batal°* |

Where can (I) buy a
  bus/train ticket?
*Di mana (saya) bisa beli
  karcis bis/kereta api?*
At the train station.
*Di setasiun kereta api.*
At the bus terminal.
*Di terminal bis.*

Where is the bus agent?
*Di mana agen bis?*
Are there still seats?
*Masih ada tempat (duduk)?*
Sorry, already full.
*Ma'af, sudah penuh.*

Where is the ticket
  window?
*Di mana loketnya?*
I want to buy a ticket to
  Yogyakarta.
*Saya mau beli karcis ke
  Yogyakarta.*

| | |
|---|---|
| How much for 2nd class? | *Berapa untuk kelas dua?* |
| How long does it take to get there (by bus)? | *Berapa lama (naik bis) ke sana?* |
| | |
| Does it go directly to Yogya (or not)? | *Bis ini pergi langsung ke Yogya, bukan?* |
| Does (it) have air-conditioning? | *Pakai AC tidak?* |
| | |
| What time does the night bus depart? | *Jam berapa bis malam berangkat?* |
| Where do we board? | *Naik dari mana?* |
| Can we board here? | *Bisa naik di sini?* |
| | |
| I want to cancel this ticket. | *Saya mau batal karcis ini.* |
| Please return my money. | *Tolong kembali uang saya.* |
| | |
| Is this an express train? | *Ini kereta api expres, bukan?* |
| Is this bus fast or slow? | *Bis ini cepat atau pelan?* |
| | |
| Taxi! To the airport! | *Taksi! Ke airport!* |
| Please go fast. | *Tolong pergi cepat.* |
| | |
| Where is the Merpati agent? | *Di mana agen Merpati?* |
| What day does the boat leave for Singapore? | *Hari apa kapal laut berangkat ke Singapura?* |
| Probably on Monday. | *Barangkali hari Senen..* |

# PUBLIC TRANSPORT

**Travel Notes and Tips:**

1. Indonesians speak of a bus <u>terminal</u> but a train <u>station</u>.
2. Train tickets have to be bought at the station, but bus tickets can be bought from an agent.
3. Bus terminals are usually far out of town, but buses can often be boarded at the agent's office. Ask first.
4. Night buses are express, most day buses are local.
5. *Bemos* are minibuses used on local routes. In some places there are intercity minibuses used for intermediate distances (e.g. Yogya—Solo), called *travel*.
6. Most comfortable spot on a bus or minibus is in the middle (*di tengah*), but not over a wheel.
7. Trains have dining cars or you can buy food at the station. Buses stop periodically for meals and calls of nature. Bring your own food on most boats.
8. Don't be in a hurry—no one else is.

## ASKING DIRECTIONS

| | | | |
|---|---|---|---|
| north | *utara* | inside | *di dalam* |
| south | *selatan* | outside | *di luar* |
| east | *timur* | in front of | *di muka/depan* |
| west | *barat* | in back of | *di belakang* |
| | | | |
| before | *sebelum* | right | *kanan* |
| after | *sesudah* | left | *kiri* |
| next to | *di sebelah* | turn | *belok* |
| far | *jauh* | near | *dekat* |

| | | | |
|---|---|---|---|
| address | *alamat* | to look for | *cari* |
| enter | *masuk* | exit, go out | *keluar* |
| road, street | *jalan* | main road | *jalan raya* |
| lane, alley | *gang* | expressway | *jalan tol* |

| | |
|---|---|
| Excuse me, Pak. | *Ma' af Pak.* |
| Where is Hotel Trio? | *Di mana Hotel Trio?* |
| Is it nearby? | *Dekat dari sini, tidak?* |
| Yes, (it is) near. | *Ya, dekat.* |

| | |
|---|---|
| How far is it? | *Berapa jauh dari sini?* |
| About two kilometers | *Kira-kira dua kilometer.* |

| | |
|---|---|
| What (are you) looking for? | *Cari apa?* |
| I am looking for this address. | *Saya cari alamat ini.* |
| It's there [pointing]. | *Di sana.* |
| How many meters from here? | *Berapa meter dari sini?* |
| About 200 meters. | *Kira-kira dua ratus meter.* |

| | |
|---|---|
| Is it on the main road? | *Ada di jalan raya?* |
| No, it is down a lane. | *Bukan, harus masuk gang.* |

| | |
|---|---|
| Go straight, then turn left at the main street. | *Jalan terus, lalu belok kiri di jalan raya.* |
| Go south, then east | *Pergi ke selatan, lalu ke timur.* |

33

# ASKING DIRECTIONS

| | |
|---|---|
| Enter the alley on the right. | *Masuk gang di sebelah kanan.* |
| (Is it) in front or in back of the house? | *(Ada) di muka atau di belakang rumah?* |
| It's in front. | *Ada di muka.* |
| It's outside. | *Ada di luar.* |
| It's to the left. | *Ada di sebelah kiri.* |
| Thank you, ma'am. | *Terima kasih, bu.* |
| You're welcome. | *Kembali.* |

**Note:** When asking directions, it's better not to use yes/no questions because people will often answer yes or no without having understood the question. Instead, ask "Where is—?" If it's an obscure place, keep asking as you go along and eventually you'll get there.

PLACES

## Geography

| | | | |
|---|---|---|---|
| world | *dunia* | mountain | *gunung* |
| island | *pulau* | volcano | *gunung api* |
| lake | *danau* | summit, peak | *puncak* |
| beach | *pantai* | sea | *laut* |
| river | *sungai, kali* | forest | *hutan* |
| country | *negara* | territory | *daerah* |

## Tourist sites  *Obyek wisata*

| | | | |
|---|---|---|---|
| park | *taman, kebun* | nature reserve | *cagar alam* |
| waterfall | *air terjun* | hot spring | *mata air panas* |
| temple | *candi* | zoo | *kebun binatang* |
| swimming pool | *kolam renang* | palace | *keraton* |
| | | museum | *musium* |

## In the city  *Dalam kota*

| | | | |
|---|---|---|---|
| city | *kota besar°* | hospital | *rumah sakit* |
| town | *kota°* | market | *pasar* |
| village | *desa* | bank | *bank* |
| downtown | *pusat kota* | mosque | *mesjid* |

| | | | |
|---|---|---|---|
| store | *toko* | hotel | *hotel* |
| cinema | *bioskop°* | lodge | *losmen* |
| university | *universitas* | guesthouse | *wisma* |
| church | *gereja* | restaurant | *rumah makan* |

| | |
|---|---|
| immigration office | *kantor immigrasi* |
| tourism office | *kantor pariwisata°* |
| embassy | *kedutaan besar, kedubes* |

## Around the house  *Di rumah*

| | | | |
|---|---|---|---|
| house | *rumah* | room | *kamar* |
| sleep | *tidur* | bedroom | *kamar tidur°* |
| bath | *mandi* | bathroom | *kamar mandi* |
| kitchen | *dapur* | toilet | *kamar kecil, WC* |

# FOOD AND DRINK

## Useful words

| | | | |
|---|---|---|---|
| to eat | *makan* | restaurant | *restoran,* |
| food | *makanan* | | *rumah makan* |
| to drink | *minum* | menu | *daftar* |
| drink | *minuman* | | *makanan* |
| tasty, nice | *enak* | waiter | *pelayan* |
| delicious | *sedap* | plate | *piring* |
| | | glass | *gelas* |
| breakfast | *makan pagi* | cup | *cangkir* |
| lunch | *makan siang* | knife | *pisau* |
| dinner | *makan malam* | fork | *garpu* |
| | | spoon | *sendok* |

## Fruits *buah-buahan*

| | | | |
|---|---|---|---|
| mango | *mangga* | pineapple | *nanas* |
| durian | *durian* | citrus | *jeruk* |
| jackfruit | *nangka* | mangosteen | *manggis* |
| coconut | *kelapa* | apple | *apel* |
| papaya | *pepaya* | banana | *pisang* |
| strawberry | *arbai, arben* | watermelon | *semangka* |

## Meat *daging*

| | | | |
|---|---|---|---|
| beef | *daging sapi°* | chicken | *daging ayam* |
| pork | *daging babi* | duck | *daging bebek°* |
| lamb | *domba°* | pigeon | *burung dara* |
| goat, | | liver | *hati* |
| mutton | *kambing* | brains | *otak* |
| | | heart | *jantung* |

## Seafood

| | | | |
|---|---|---|---|
| ocean fish | *ikan laut* | lake fish | *ikan danau* |
| lobster | *udang karang* | squid | *cumi-cumi* |
| oysters | *tiram* | shrimp, | |
| crab | *kepiting°* | prawns | *udang* |

## For vegetarians

| | |
|---|---|
| without meat | *tanpa° daging* |
| only vegetables | *sayur saja* |

## Staples

| | |
|---|---|
| rice | *nasi* |
| noodles | *mie, bihun, bakmi* |
| bread | *roti* |

## Snacks *jajan*

| | |
|---|---|
| cake | *kue* |
| candy, (sweets) | *permen, gula-gula* |
| peanuts | *kacang* |

## Condiments/flavor

| | | | |
|---|---|---|---|
| hot/warm | *panas* | chili | *lombok, cabe°* |
| hot/spicy | *pedas* | salt | *garam* |
| cold | *dingin°* | pepper | *merica, lada* |
| sweet | *manis* | soya sauce | *kecap* |
| sour | *asam* | butter | *mentega* |
| salty | *asin°* | honey | *madu* |

# FOOD AND DRINK

## Prepared dishes

There are many local dishes in Indonesia, with a great deal of regional variation. Here is a brief listing of some common ones. C = Chinese origin; M = Middle Eastern.

| | |
|---|---|
| *nasi putih* | steamed white rice |
| *nasi goreng* | fried rice, sometimes with vegetable, egg and meat |
| *nasi rames* | plate of rice with side dishes, including vegetable and meat |
| *mie goreng* | fried noodles, sometimes with vegetables |
| *mie* | noodles |
| *mie kuah* | served in stock, with vegetables |
| *soto, sop* | soup, often spicy with meat |
| *sate* | broiled meat on skewers, with peanut sauce |
| *gulai* (M) | meat in curry broth |
| *martabak* | meat/onion pancake, fried |
| *cap cay* (C) | stir fried vegetables and meat |
| *fu yong hai* (C) | vegetable and meat omelette |
| *pangsit* (C) | wonton dumplings |
| *bakso* (C) | meatballs (usually beef) |
| *gado-gado* | veg. salad with peanut sauce |
| *telur* | egg |
| — *rebus* | — boiled |
| — *goreng* | — fried (both sides) |
| — *mata sapi* | — "sunny side up" (lit: "cow's eye") |

## Drinks

| | | | |
|---|---|---|---|
| hot | *panas°* | ginger tea | *jahe* |
| cold | *dingin°* | chocolate | *coklat* |
| ice | *es°* | sweet | *manis* |
| bottle | *botol* | bitter | *pahit* |
| water | *air* | only a little | *sedikit saja* |
| boiled water | *air putih* | sugar | *gula* |
| milk | *susu* | without sugar | *tanpa° gula* |
| coffee | *kopi* | beer | *bir* |
| tea | *teh* | cordial | *strop* |

soft drinks (by brand name):   Coca Cola, Fanta, etc.)

## Blended fruit drinks   *es jus* + fruit name

## Other fruit drinks

| | |
|---|---|
| *es jeruk* | iced lemon/orange juice, sweetened |
| *es kelapa* | iced coconut milk |
| *es kelapa muda* | iced young coconut milk + 'meat' and sugar syrup |
| *es kopior* | iced overripe coconut milk + 'meat' and sugar syrup |
| *es buah* | jelly-like fruits and syrup on ice served in a bowl |
| *es kacang* | shaved ice with sugar syrup over a bowl of beans and jellies |
| *ronde* | a spicy hot drink served in a bowl at some warungs |

# BARGAINING

Buying and bargaining in Indonesian can be fun or it can be tremendously frustrating, depending largely on your attitude. There are three "buying situations" here:

1. **Fixed Prices:** Sometimes the prices are really fixed, meaning no reductions. This is usually the case in medium and large hotels, restaurants, department and other large stores. If you see the price posted, that's usually it.

2. **Polite Wrangling:** This applies anytime you're making a major purchase in a medium size or smaller store, even if the price is posted or you see a "Harga Pas" sign. Always ask for a reduction if you are buying something big. Indonesians do. For major purchases you should take your time, chat with the shopkeepers and be friendly. Usually you will get 10% off at the very least. Sometimes you'll get much more than that. Never act overly eager or in a rush to buy! Keep pointing out the (real or imagined) defects of the thing you are buying.

3. **Bargaining:** This applies to markets, beach or street vendors of tourist items, pedicabs (*becaks*), Sumatran buses (usually), souvenir shops and anyone who quotes you an outrageous price for something. This is more of an open contest, but remember it's a game you'll win by strategy, not by anger or intimidation. Always keep your cool. Here are some winning strategies:

# BARGAINING

A. Know the right price (*harga pas*) **before** you buy. How? Compare prices first and learn about the different qualities of goods. And ask an Indonesian who is unconnected with the goods or services being offered. Indonesians are always exchanging price information so **they** don't pay too much. They will be happy to tell you.

B. Make the first bid. If you know the right price, or have a good idea, make a first bid that is lower than the correct price rather than asking the price. This gets you off to a more realistic start, as the seller then knows that you know how much it should cost.

C. The walk away. A must with *becaks*. Anytime you think you've offered a good price, just smile, shrug your shoulders, and walk away slowly, repeating the price. Often the seller will call you back, agreeing to your offer. Once the seller has agreed, you must buy. It is very bad to renege and the seller may rightfully get very angry. So never make an offer you don't intend to go through with, no matter how low it may seem!

D. Use your Indonesian! The more fluent you are, the easier bargaining becomes.

E. Always keep smiling! Never get angry or act insulted by a high price. This gets you nowhere. There is no concept of a 'right' price or 'overcharging' in Indonesia. If you paid too much, it's your own fault.

# SHOPPING

**Useful words**

| | | | |
|---|---|---|---|
| to buy | *beli* | cheap | *murah* |
| to sell | *jual* | expensive | *mahal* |
| to bargain | *tawar* | too much | *terlalu* |
| to lose money | *rugi* | | *banyak* |
| price | *harga* | less, reduce | *kurang* |
| quality | *kwalitet°* | kind, type | *macam* |
| cost | *ongkos* | color | *warna* |
| money | *uang* | buy a lot | *borong* |
| shop | *toko* | market | *pasar* |

| | |
|---|---|
| 'usual' price | *harga biasa* |
| fixed price, net price | *harga pas* |
| 'just looking' | *lihat-lihat saja* |
| How much (is the price)? | *Berapa (harganya)?* |

BUYING FRUIT AT THE MARKET
F = foreigner,  IB = Indonesian bystander,  S = seller

| | | |
|---|---|---|
| F: | Excuse me, Sir. What is the usual price of that fruit? (pointing) | *Ma'af, Pak. Berapa harga biasa buah itu?* |
| IB: | About Rp 2.000 per kilo. | *Kira-kira dua ribu rupiah per kilo.* |
| F: | (walks over) Good morning, Bu. I want to buy a kilo of | *Selamat pagi, Bu. Saya mau beli satu kilo buah ini untuk* |

|  |  |  |
|---|---|---|
|  | this fruit for Rp 1.600. | *seribu enam ratus rupiah.* |
| S: | No can. I lose. Price of this is Rp 3.000 per kilo. | *Tak bisa. Saya rugi. Harga ini tiga ribu rupiah se kilo (se = satu).* |
| F: | (smile!) Too expensive. Rp 2.000 is the usual price. | *Terlalu mahal. Harga biasa dua ribu.* |
| S: | Yes, okay. | *Ya, boleh.* |

IN A STORE

|  |  |  |
|---|---|---|
| F: | What's the price of this? | *Berapa harga ini?* |
| S: | That's Rp 50.000, sir. | *Itu lima puluh ribu rupiah, tuan.* |
| F: | That's expensive! Can you reduce it? | *Mahal! Bisa kurang?* |
| S: | Yes, a little. | *Bisa, sedikit.* |
| F: | Do you have many kinds? | *Ada banyak macam?* |
| S: | Yes, and many qualities. | *Ya, dan banyak kwalitet.* |
| F: | May I see? | *Boleh saya lihat?* |
| S: | This color is nice. | *Warna ini bagus.* |
| F: | Can (you) reduce the price if I buy two? | *Bisa kurang kalau saya beli dua?* |
| S: | Sorry, it's a fixed price. | *Ma'af. Itu harga pas.* |

43

# SHOPPING

| F: | Today I'm just looking; maybe I'll come back tomorrow. | *Hari ini saya lihat-lihat saja; mungkin saya kembali besok.* |

## Things to buy

| jewelry | *intan permata* |
|---|---|
| silver | *perak* |
| gold | *mas* |
| | |
| wood | *kayu* |
| leather | *kulit* |
| bone | *tulang* |
| horn | *tanduk* |
| ivory | *gading* |
| | |
| masks | *topeng* |
| paintings | *lukisan* |
| woodcarvings | *ukiran kayu* |
| tablecloths | *taplak meja°* |
| bedspreads | *seperai°* |
| bags | *tas°* |
| fabric | *kain* |
| wayang puppets | *wayang kulit* |
| leather goods | *barang kulit* |

| | |
|---|---|
| clothing | *pakaian* |
| long cloth (2 meters) | *kain panjang* |
| sarong-length cloth | *kain sarung* |
| blouse, shirt | *kemeja* |
| T-shirt | *kaus* |
| dress, skirt | *rok* |
| | |
| handdrawn batik | *batik tulis* |
| copper-stamped batik | *batik cap* |
| print (not batik) | *sablon* |

## A few more terms and phrases

| | |
|---|---|
| to try on | *mencoba* |
| May I try on this dress? | *Boleh saya mencoba rok ini?* |
| | |
| factory | *pabrik* |
| to make | *bikin, membuat* |
| | |
| Which place makes hand-drawn batik? | *Tempat yang mana membuat batik tulis?* |
| | |
| made | *dibuat* |
| Where are these goods made? | *Barang-barang ini dibuat di mana?* |

# AT THE HOTEL

| | |
|---|---|
| room | *kamar°* |
| empty | *kosong* |
| full | *penuh* |
| follow | *ikut* |
| blanket | *selimut* |
| sheet | *seperai°* |
| pillow | *bantal* |
| to deposit | *titip* |
| to wash (clothes) | *mencuci* |
| to clean | *bikin bersih* |
| to spray | *semprot°* |
| mosquito | *nyamuk* |
| key, lock | *kunci* |
| receptionist | *resepsionis* |

| | |
|---|---|
| Still have an empty room? | *Masih ada kamar kosong?* |
| For one or two persons, sir? | *Untuk satu atau dua orang, tuan?* |
| Two people. | *Dua orang.* |
| Yes, there is. | *Ya, ada.* |
| May I see (it)? | *Boleh saya lihat?* |
| Yes, please follow me. | *Ya, silakan ikut saya.* |

| | |
|---|---|
| This is fine. | *Ini boleh.* |
| How much for one night? | *Berapa untuk satu malam?* |
| May I deposit my passport with you? | *Boleh saya titip paspor saya dengan anda?* |
| Is there someone who washes clothes? | *Ada orang yang mencuci pakaian?* |
| Please spray my room. | *Tolong semprot kamar saya.* |
| There are some mosquitoes inside. | *Ada nyamuk di dalam.* |
| Please clean my room. | *Tolong bikin bersih kamar saya.* |
| I'm leaving tomorrow midday. | *Saya berangkat besok siang.* |
| Goodbye. (to person leaving) | *Selamat jalan.* |
| Goodbye. (to person staying) | *Selamat tinggal.* |

# AT THE POST OFFICE

| post office | *kantor pos°* | postcard | *kartu pos* |
| central | *pusat* | send | *kirim* |
| branch | *cabang* | package | *paket* |
| airmail | *pos udara* | stamp | *perangko* |
| letter | *surat* | register | *tercatat°* |
| aerogram | *aerogramme* | telegram | *kawat* |

*ekspres* — express service for international airmail.

*kilat* — express service within Indonesia

*kilat khusus* — special registered delivery within Indonesia

| I want to send this letter to England. | *Saya mau kirim surat ini ke negeri Inggeris.* |
| (Do you) want to send it airmail? | *Mau kirim pos udara?* |
| Yes, and express. | *Ya, dan ekspres.* |
| Rp 1.500. | *Seribu lima ratus rupiah.* |
| Thank you. | *Terima kasih.* |

# AT THE POST OFFICE

| | |
|---|---|
| You're welcome. | *Kembali.* |
| I want to pick up (take) a registered letter. | *Saya mau ambil surat tercatat.* |
| I want to send this letter by *kilat khusus* to Jakarta. | *Saya mau kirim surat ini kilat khusus ke Jakarta.* |
| The cost is Rp 3.000. | *Ongkosnya tiga ribu rupiah.* |
| Where is the telegram office? | *Di mana kantor telegram?* |
| Next door. | *Di sebelah.* |

**Helpful tips:**
- Express service costs extra and usually saves 1-2 days.
- Register anything of value.
- If possible, watch the stamps being cancelled.
- Telegrams sent to points within Indonesia are very cheap and fast.

| | |
|---|---|
| healthy | *sehat* |
| sick | *sakit* |
| doctor | *dokter* |
| hospital | *rumah sakit* |
| | |
| medicine, drug | *obat* |
| pharmacy | *apotik°* |
| diarrhea | *berak-berak* |
| | |
| flu | *flu°, pilek* |
| to call | *panggil* |
| | |
| broken leg | *kaki patah* |
| broken arm | *lengan patah* |
| to bring | *bawa* |
| | |
| cold | *masuk angin* |
| to vomit | *muntah* |
| fever | *demam* |
| cholera | *kolera* |
| infection | *infeksi* |
| malaria | *malaria* |
| | |
| injection | *suntik* |

I'm sick. Is there a doctor near here?

*Saya sakit. Ada dokter di dekat sini?*

Where is the best hospital?

*Di mana rumah sakit yang paling baik.*

Please buy medicine for me at the pharmacy.

*Tolong beli obat untuk saya di apotik.*

I need medicine for diarrhea.

*Saya perlu obat untuk berak-berak.*

I'm sick (with) flu.

*Saya sakit flu.*

Please call a taxi.

*Tolong panggil taksi.*

Help! My friend's leg is broken.

*Tolong! Kaki teman saya patah.*

Bring us to a hospital.

*Bawa kami ke rumah sakit.*

# AT THE BANK

| | |
|---|---|
| to exchange | *tukar* |
| traveler's checks | (same) |
| exchange rate | *kurs* |
| dollar | *dolar°* |
| | |
| transfer | *transfer* |
| not yet | *belum* |
| to contact | *hubungi* |
| branch office | *cabang* |
| | |
| money | *uang* |
| cash | *uang tunai, uang kontan* |

Excuse me, Miss. Where can I exchange traveler's checks?

*Ma'af, Nona. Di mana bisa saya tukar traveler's checks?*

I want to exchange American dollars.

*Saya mau tukar dolar Amerika.*

What is the rate of exchange today?

*Berapa kurs dolar hari ini?*

Rp 2.000 for one dollar.

*Dua ribu rupiah untuk satu dolar.*

| | |
|---|---|
| O.K. I'll change $50. | *Baik. Saya mau tukar lima puluh dolar.* |
| Is there a transfer for me? My name is Humbert. | *Ada transfer untuk saya? Nama saya Humbert.* |
| I'm sorry, (it) hasn't arrived yet. | *Ma'af, belum datang.* |
| This transfer is already one week late. | *Transfer ini sudah terlambat satu minggu.* |
| Please contact the Jakarta branch for me. | *Tolong hubungi cabang Jakarta untuk saya.* |
| I'll return the day after tomorrow. | *Saya kembali lagi besok lusa.* |

**Helpful tip:** If someone transfers money to you from abroad, ask them to use an international bank and to mail you a copy of the transfer notice separately.

| | |
|---|---|
| business | *dagang* |
| import(er) | *impor(tir)* |
| export(er) | *expor(tir)* |
| supplier | *supplier, grosir* |
| customer | *langganan* |
| wholesale price | *harga borongan* |
| profit | *untung, laba* |
| quantity | *jumlah* |
| piece, unit | *potong, buah* |
| sample | *contoh* |
| to order | *pesan* |
| | |
| shipment | *pengiriman* |
| shipping agent | *ekspedisi* |
| to send | *kirim* |
| to pack | *membungkus* |
| package | *bungkus, paket* |
| insurance | *assuransi* |

Who is the exporter of these goods?
*Siapa yang jadi exportir barang ini?*

Where is the best supplier?
*Di mana supplier yang paling baik?*

Which supplier is the biggest?
*Grosir mana yang paling besar?*

# BUSINESS/SENDING GOODS

I request the wholesale price for this batik.
*Saya minta harga borongan untuk batik ini.*

How many pieces can you make per month?
*Berapa potong anda bisa membuat per bulan?*

I need three samples of this type.
*Saya perlu tiga contoh seperti ini.*

I want to order 300 pieces.
*Saya mau pesan tiga ratus potong.*

I want to send these goods to Australia.
*Saya mau kirim barang ini ke Australia.*

Which shipping agent is the best?
*Expedisi mana yang paling baik?*

I want to send this shipment in two days.
*Saya mau kirim pengiriman ini dalam dua hari.*

Who can pack them for me?
*Siapa bisa membungkus ini untuk saya?*

Please make a very strong package.
*Tolong bikin bungkus yang kuat sekali.*

Do I need insurance?
*Apakah saya perlu assuransi?*

# SWIMMING & EXPLORING

| | |
|---|---|
| beach | *pantai* |
| beautiful | *indah* (place) |
| | *cantik* (women) |
| also | *juga* |
| wave | *ombak* |
| sand | *pasir* |
| safe | *aman* |
| to swim | *berenang* |
| cave | *gua* |
| hot springs | *mata air panas* |
| waterfall | *air terjun* |
| to climb | *naik, mendaki* |
| summit, top | *puncak* |
| volcano | *gunung api* |
| to reach | *sampai* |
| to the top | *ke atas* |

This beach (is) very beautiful.   *Pantai ini indah sekali.*
That girl (is) also beautiful.   *Gadis itu juga cantik.*

I like big waves    *Saya suka ombak besar*
  and white sand.      *dan pasir putih.*

(Is it) safe to swim here?   *Aman tidak berenang*
     *di sini?*

| | |
|---|---|
| Yes, but don't swim too far. | *Ya, tetapi jangan berenang terlalu jauh.* |
| Is there a cave near here? | *Ada gua dekat sini?* |
| There are two near the hot spring. | *Ada dua dekat mata air panas.* |
| Where is the waterfall? | *Di mana ada air terjun?* |
| Half a kilometer to the east. | *Setengah kilometer ke timur.* |
| I want to climb to the top of that volcano. | *Saya mau naik ke puncak gunung api itu.* |
| From where can (one) climb up? | *Dari mana bisa mendaki?* |
| From a village on the north side. | *Dari desa di sebelah utara.* |
| How long does it take to reach the summit? | *Berapa lama untuk sampai di puncak?* |

# SMALL TALK

| | |
|---|---|
| to go for a walk | *jalan-jalan* |
| to originate, come from | *asal* |
| (to have) ever | *(sudah) pernah* |
| already | *sudah* |
| married | *kawin* |
| original | *asli* |
| practice | *latihan* |
| to learn | *belajar* |
| foreigner | *orang asing* |
| age | *umur* |

| | |
|---|---|
| Hello. What's your name? | *Hello. Siapa namanya?* |
| Lolita. What's your name? | *Lolita. Siapa nama bapak?* |
| My name's Peter. | *Nama saya Peter.* |
| Where are you going? | *Mau ke mana?* |
| Just taking a walk. | *Jalan-jalan saja.* |
| Where (do you) come from? | *Asal dari mana?* |
| Switzerland. | *Swiss.* |

| | |
|---|---|
| How long (have you) been here? (=Already how long here?) | *Sudah berapa lama di sini?* |
| One month. | *Satu bulan.* |

| | |
|---|---|
| (Are you) already married (or not)? | *Sudah kawin belum?* |
| Yes. Four times. | *Ya. Empat kali.* |
| | |
| (Have you) ever been to Bali? | *Sudah pernah ke Bali?* |
| Yes, already. | *Ya, sudah.* |
| | |
| May I practice English with you? | *Boleh saya latihan Bahasa Inggeris dengan anda?* |
| O.K. I want to learn Indonesian. | *Baik. Saya mau belajar Bahasa Indonesia.* |
| | |
| I'm sorry. Perhaps another time. | *Ma'af sekali. Mungkin lain waktu.* |

**Cultural note:** Indonesians have a great love of togetherness and "small talk" (*obrol*) which often clashes with Western notions of privacy. They are also very curious about foreigners and want to be able to place you by knowing where you are from, what your religion is, whether you are married, how many children you have, how long you are staying, etc. Realize that this is a cultural difference and be diplomatic in not answering questions you consider too personal. Evasiveness is an acceptable way of turning aside questions.

# EXPRESSIONS

These three phrases refer to going for a stroll and are good answers to the perennial question: *Mau ke mana?* (Where are you going?)

| | |
|---|---|
| *makan angin* | "eat wind" |
| *cari angin* | "look for wind" |
| *cuci mata* | "wash eyes" |

Other phrases :

| | | |
|---|---|---|
| *masuk angin* | "enter wind" | to catch a cold |
| *main-main* | "play-play" | As in *Main-main ke rumah kalau ada waktu* = Come play/visit my house when you have the time. |
| *aduh!* | | an expression of surprise or pain |
| *kepala udang* | "prawn head" | idiot |
| *jam karet* | "rubber time" | |

# FILLING OUT FORMS

**Useful words**

| | |
|---|---|
| *nama* | name |
| *alamat* | address |
| *alamat lengkap* | complete adress |
| *tanggal (tgl)* | date |
| *tanggal lahir* | date of birth |
| *tempat lahir* | place of birth |
| *umur* | age |
| | |
| *kebangsaan* | nationality |
| *surat keterangan* | identification papers |
| *nomor paspor* | passport number |
| *maksud kunjungan* | purpose of visit |
| *pekerjaan* | profession |
| | |
| *agama* | religion |
| *kawin* | marital status |

# GLOSSARY

## A

| | |
|---|---|
| about | *kira-kira* |
| after | *sesudah* |
| age | *umur* |
| ago | *yang lalu* |
| airport | *airport* |
| alone | *sendiri* |
| already | *sudah* |
| also | *juga* |
| always | *selalu* |
| and | *dan* |
| answer (v.) | *jawab* |
| art | *kesenian* |
| ask | *tanya* |

## B

| | |
|---|---|
| bargain | *tawar* |
| beautiful | *indah, cantik* |
| belief | *keper-cayaan* |
| believe | *percaya* |
| bicycle | *sepeda, basikal°* |
| big | *besar* |
| book | *buku* |

| | |
|---|---|
| bother | *ganggu* |
| bring | *membawa* |
| broken | *rusak* |
| but | *tetapi* |
| buy | *beli* |

## C

| | |
|---|---|
| can | *bisa, boleh°* |
| cancel | *batal, hapus°* |
| call | *panggil* |
| car | *mobil, kereta°* |
| careful | *hati-hati* |
| central | *pusat* |
| cheap | *murah* |
| cheat (v.) | *menipu* |
| city | *kota, negri°* |
| clean | *bersih* |
| clever | *pintar* |
| cloth | *kain* |
| clothes | *pakaian* |
| cold | *dingin, sejuk°* |
| color | *warna* |
| connection | *hubungan* |

| | |
|---|---|
| contents | *isinya* |
| continue | *jalan terus* |
| correct | *betul* |
| custom | *adat* |

## D

| | |
|---|---|
| date | *tanggal* |
| day | *hari* |
| deliver | *sampaikan* |
| deposit (v.) | *titip, simpan°* |
| difficult | *susah* |
| dirty | *kotor* |
| discount | *korting, diskaun°* |
| disturb | *ganggu* |
| drink (v.) | *minum* |

## E

| | |
|---|---|
| earlier | *tadi* |
| easy | *mudah* |
| eat | *makan* |
| emergency | *keadaan darurat* |
| empty | *kosong* |

| | |
|---|---|
| enter | *masuk* |
| except | *kecuali* |
| expensive | *mahal* |
| extra-ordinary | *luar biasa* |

## F

| | |
|---|---|
| far | *jauh* |
| father | *bapak, ayah* |
| fill | *mengisi* |
| film | *pilem* |
| find | *mendapat* |
| food | *makanan* |
| for | *untuk* |
| full | *penuh* |

## G

| | |
|---|---|
| give | *memberi* |
| go | *pergi* |
| gold | *mas* |
| good | *baik* |
| guest | *tamu* |
| guide | *perantara* |

# GLOSSARY

## H

| | |
|---|---|
| happy | *senang* |
| have | *punya* |
| he | *dia* |
| help | *tolong, bantu* |
| honest | *jujur* |
| hope (n.) | *harapan* |
| (v.) | *mengharap* |
| hospital | *rumah sakit* |
| hot | *panas* |
| hour | *jam, pukul* |
| how | *bagaimana* |

## I

| | |
|---|---|
| I | *saya* |
| if | *kalau, jika* |
| inform | *beritahu* |
| inside | *didalam* |
| interesting | *menarik* |
| into | *kedalam* |

## J

| | |
|---|---|
| jewel | *permata* |
| join | *menyusul* |
| job | *pekerjaan* |

## K

| | |
|---|---|
| key | *kunci* |
| king | *raja* |
| knife | *pisau* |
| know | *tahu* |

## L

| | |
|---|---|
| late | *terlambat* |
| later | *nanti* |
| laugh | *ketawa* |
| lazy | *malas* |
| left (adj.) | *kiri* |
| letter | *surat* |
| license | *izin* |
| lie | *bohong* |
| light (adj.) | *ringgan* |
| like | *suka* |
| lock | *kunci* |
| look for | *mencari* |
| lost | *hilang* |
| loud | *kéras* |

love     *cinta*

# M

| | |
|---|---|
| many | *banyak* |
| market | *pasar* |
| maybe | *barangkali* |
| minute | *menit* |
| money | *uang* |
| month | *bulan* |
| monument | *tugu* |
| more | *lagi* |
| mother | *ibu* |
| motorcycle | *sepeda motor* |
| must | *harus* |

# N

| | |
|---|---|
| need | *perlu* |
| new | *baru* |
| nice | *bagus* |
| no | *tidak* |
| nonsense | *omong kosong* |
| not yet | *belum* |
| now | *sekarang* |

# O

| | |
|---|---|
| often | *sering* |
| old | *tua* |
| only | *hanya* |
| order (n.) | *pesanan* |
| open | *buka* |

# P

| | |
|---|---|
| pillow | *bantal* |
| place | *tempat* |
| poor | *miskin* |
| possession | *milik* |
| possible | *mungkin* |
| practical | *praktis* |
| practice | *latihan* |
| precise | *tepat* |
| prefer | *lebih suka* |
| present (n.) | *hadiah* |
| price | *harga* |
| private | *pribadi* |
| promise | *janji* |
| prompt | *cepat* |
| pull | *tarik* |
| purpose | *maksud* |
| push | *dorong* |

# GLOSSARY

## Q

| quality | kualitet, kualiti° |
|---|---|
| queen | ratu |

## R

| read | membaca |
|---|---|
| refined | alus |
| religion | agama |
| rent (v.) | menyewa |
| repair | perbaiki |
| return | kembali |
| rich | kaya |
| right (direction) | kanan |
| road | jalan |
| room | kamar, bilik° |
| rotten | busuk |
| rule (n.) | peraturan |
| run | lari |

## S

| same | sama |
|---|---|
| see | lihat |

| she | dia |
|---|---|
| short | pendek |
| show (v.) | menunjuk |
| sick | sakit |
| small | kecil |
| song | lagu |
| so-so | lumayan |
| speak | bicara, bercakap° |
| spicy | pedas |
| store, shop | toko, kedai° |
| strong | kuat |
| stupid | bodoh |
| sweet | manis |

## T

| take | ambil |
|---|---|
| tasty | enak, sedap° |
| tell | bilang |
| temple | pura, candi |
| they | mereka |
| that | itu |
| this | ini |

| | |
|---|---|
| today | *hari ini* |
| together | *bersama* |
| toilet | *kamar kecil* |
| tomorrow | *besok* |
| trip (n.) | *perjalanan* |
| true | *benar* |
| try | *coba* |
| type (n.) | *jenis* |

## U

| | |
|---|---|
| under | *dibawa* |
| understand | *mengerti* |
| urgent | *perlu sekali* |

## V

| | |
|---|---|
| value | *nilai* |
| vehicle | *kendaraan* |
| very | *sekali* |
| view (n.) | *pemandangan* |
| village | *desa* |
| visit (n.) | *kunjungan* |
| volcano | *gunung api* |

## W

| | |
|---|---|
| wait | *tunggu* |
| want | *mau* |
| warm | *panas* |
| we | *kita, kami* |
| weak | *lemah* |
| what | *apa* |
| when | *kapan, bila°* |
| where (at) | *demana* |
| wish | *ingin* |
| who | *siapa* |
| why | *mengapa* |
| wrong | *salah* |

## X, Y, Z

| | |
|---|---|
| year | *tahun* |
| yesterday | *kemarin, semalam°* |
| you | *saudara, kamu* |
| young | *muda* |
| zoo | *kebun binatang* |

***Note:* ° indicates Malay**

67

# APPENDIX: MALAY

The following section-by-section guide lists differences in usage between Indonesian and Malay.

| Section | English | Indonesian° | Malay |
|---|---|---|---|
| **Grammar** | Miss | *Nona* | *Saudari* |
| | Mrs. | *Nyonya* | *Puan* |
| **Questions** | when | *kapan* | *bila* |
| **Time** | hour | *jam, pukul* | *pukul*(only) |
| | afternoon | *sore* | *petang* |
| | yesterday | *kemarin* | *semalam* |
| | 7:30 | *setengah delapan* | *tujuh setengah* |
| | 2:45 | *tiga kurang seperempat* | *dua empat puluh lima minit* |
| **W & S I** | can | *bisa* | *boleh* |
| **W & S II** | speak | *bicara* | *bercakap* |
| | tell | *bilang* | *beritahu* |
| **Getting Around** | car | *mobil* | *kereta* |
| | bicycle | *sepeda* | *basikal* |
| | motorcycle | *sepeda motor* | *motosikal* |
| **Public Transport** | station | *setasiun* | *perhentian* |
| | ticket | *karcis* | *tiket* |
| | ticket window | *loket* | *tempat tiket* |
| | bus | *bis* | *bus* |
| | cancel | *batal* | *hapus* |
| **Places** | city | *kota besar* | *negri, bandar* |
| | town | *kota* | *pekan* |
| | office | *kantor* | *office* |
| | tourist | *pariwisata* | *pelancung* |

|  | | | |
|---|---|---|---|
| | cinema | *bioskop* | *panggung* |
| | room | *kamar* | *bilik* |
| | bedroom | *kamar tidur* | *bilik tidur* |
| | bathroom | *kamar mandi* | *bilik mandi* |
| | toilet | *kamar kecil* | *tandas* |
| | store | *toko* | *kedai* |
| | pharmacy | *apotik* | *kedai ubat* |
| | petrol station | *pompa bensin* | *stesen pump minyak* |
| **Food & Drink** | beef | *daging sapi* | *daging lembu* |
| | lamb | *domba* | *kambing biri-biri* |
| | duck | *bebek* | *itek* |
| | without... | *tanpa...* | *tidak pakai...* |
| | crab | *kepiting* | *ketam* |
| | cold | *dingin* | *sejuk* |
| | salty | *asin* | *masin* |
| | chili | *lombok* | *lada* |
| | ice | *es* | *air batu* |
| **Shopping** | quality | *kwalitet* | *jenis bahan* |
| | bag | *tas* | *beg* |
| | tablecloth | *taplak meja* | *kain meja* |
| | bedspread | *seperai* | *kain cadar* |
| **Hotel** | room | *kamar* | *bilik* |
| | sheet | *seperai* | *cadar* |
| | to spray | *semprot* | *sembur* |
| **Post** | post office | *kantor pos* | *pejabat pos* |
| | to register | *tercatat* | *kiriman khas* |
| **Health** | flu | *flu* | *demam kepialu* |
| **Bank** | dollar | *dolar* | *ringgit* |

# BODY LANGUAGE

**When you're smiling** — Indonesians are great smilers. You'll get more smiles on a streetcorner here than on one in any Western city. A smile conveys goodwill, smooths over conflicts, bridges language and culture gaps. It's also said the Indonesians have a smile for every emotion, so don't be misled.

**"Come here"** is not conveyed by the crooked index finger — instead the hand is extended palm down and the fingers are waved downward.

**The left hand** is considered unclean. For touching people or receiving or giving things, it's best to use the right hand.

**The feet** are the lowest part of the body; as a rule it's very rude to put them up in the air or point them at people when sitting.

**Aggressive gestures** and postures are disdained, including pointing directly at someone, crossing arms over chest, and standing with hands on hips.